CU00701131

Rough Magic & Smock Alley Theatre present

ALL THE ANGELS
(HANDEL AND THE FIRST MESSIAH)
by NICK DRAKE

This production premiered at
Smock Alley Theatre, Dublin on 23 November 2021.

All The Angels was first produced at
The Globe Theatre in London on 26 June 2015.

ROUGH
MAGIC

Rough Magic is one of Ireland's leading theatre producers and a significant mentor of emerging artists. It provides an unexpected angle to the mainstream and an anchor to the emerging generation.

Since its foundation in 1984, Rough Magic has produced 134 shows, including 39 Irish premieres and 30 World Premieres. With 37 continuous years in the field of theatre production and touring, Rough Magic is recognised both as an independent creative entity and a valued institution. We operate as an ensemble across a wide spectrum of scale and style, covering international contemporary work, world classics and new Irish writing, with the audience at the heart of everything we do.

In 2021 the company launched COMPASS, folding play development and support for emerging theatre artists into the company's core programming. COMPASS will develop partnerships to produce major new commissions as we approach our 40th Anniversary and support artists at every level.

Awards include: a record four Irish Times Irish Theatre Awards for Best Production (*Copenhagen* 2003, *Improbable Frequency* 2005, *The Taming of the Shrew* 2007, *Don Carlos* 2008); London Time Out Award; two Edinburgh Fringe First Awards and the Irish Times Irish Theatre Award for Best Ensemble for *A Midsummer Night's Dream* in 2018.

Smock Alley Theatre lies in an unassuming part of Dublin city. Nestled on the banks of the River Liffey it was originally built in 1662, The Theatre Royal at Smock Alley gave the world the plays of George Farquhar (*The Recruiting Officer*), Oliver Goldsmith (*She Stoops to Conquer*) and Richard Brinsley Sheridan (*The Rivals*). 300 people attended the theatre each night, seven days a week, to be enthralled, entertained and enlightened by actors, acrobats, dancers, musicians and trapeze artists. Hundreds of candles blazed in brass chandeliers as Peg Woffington, Charles Macklin, Rachel Baptiste and even the greatest actor of his generation, David Garrick, trod the boards of one of the finest theatres in the Kingdom.

Sadly through old age, rival theatres and a number of new found structural problems, the once great theatre fell into disrepair and disfavour in the city. The great doors closed in 1787 and the building found a new lease of life as a Catholic Church from 1811 - 1989 a fate which preserved the structure and maintained its connection with the local community.

Now, 350 years after it was first built, the theatre has been carefully and lovingly restored to become Dublin's Oldest Newest Theatre. It is once again a bustling hub of theatre, song, dance, art and creativity.

Within the walls of the new Smock Alley you will find two theatres, a unique Banquet Hall, space for creativity, and programmes for artist development. The theatre is now a vital resource within the ecology of Irish theatre, supporting artists, companies and festivals. Through our Scene & Heard festival of new work and supportive development programmes we are often the first professional engagement for young theatre artists.

We are creating a self-sustaining loop where work on the stage inspires development, rehearsal, creativity, connections, and support that foster the talent and skills that will once again feed back onto the stage.

'I just adore it as a theatre, the tickets are always affordable and just the experience of being in that building is magical even before the show begins'

FOR SMOCK ALLEY THEATRE

Director	Patrick Sutton
Director of Programming & Finance	Lucy Ryan
General Manager	Paul Clune
Technical Manager	Dave Halpin
Box Office & Marketing Manager	Osgar Dukes
Event Manager	Sarah O'Neill
Technical Team	Ross McSherry, Brian Nutley
Box Office	Emily Fox
Front of House Team	Sarah Foley
	Mark O'Reilly
	Ella Scally
	Ashlynn O'Neill
	Ceara Carney
	Matt McGowan
	James Hudson
	Sebastian Daly Wall
Board of Directors	Brendan Lynott (Chair)
	Danielle Fleming
	Brendan Phelan
	Fiona Ni Mhaile
	Gerry Demsey
	Mark Lambert

Smock Alley Theatre wish to acknowledge the support of
A&L Goodbody throughout the year.

A&L Goodbody

Rough Magic & Smock Alley Theatre present

ALL THE ANGELS
(HANDEL AND THE FIRST MESSIAH)
by NICK DRAKE

CAST

George Frideric Handel	Brian Doherty
Crazy Crow / Charles Burney / Jennens / Cavendish	Ross Gaynor
Susannah Cibber	Rebecca O'Mara
Soprano / Signora Avoglio	Megan O'Neill
Tenor	Ross Scanlon
Baritone	Owen Gilhooly-Miles

Director	Lynne Parker
Musical Director	Hélène Montague
Music and Recording Supervisor	Cathal Synnott
Set and Lighting Designer	Sarah Jane Shiels
Costume Designer	Sorcha Ni Fhloinn
Sound Designer	Fiona Sheil
Hair and Make Up	Val Sherlock
Assistant Director	Dominic O'Brien

Production Manager	Rob Furey
Stage Manager	Mark Jackson
Assistant Stage Manager	Nicole Darragh
Costume Supervisor	Iseult Deane
Chief LX	Eoin Winning
Sound Technician	John Norton

Producers	Sara Cregan | Rough Magic Lucy Ryan | Smock Alley
Digital Marketing	Aileen Power
Publicity	Jenny Sharif
Graphic Design	Gareth Jones

Nick Drake
Author

Nick Drake is a poet, screenwriter, and playwright. *The Man in the White Suit* (Bloodaxe) was a Poetry Society Recommendation and won the Waterstones/Forward Prize for Best First Collection. It was followed by *From The Word Go* (Bloodaxe) and *The Farewell Glacier* (Bloodaxe), a book-length poem about the climate emergency in the Arctic inspired by a voyage around the Svalbard archipelago. *The Farewell Glacier* was recorded for *High Arctic* (National Maritime Museum), an award-winning installation by United Visual Artists; and dramatised at COP 26 (Glasgow), performed by Peter Mullan. He also collaborated with UVA on *Message from the Unseen World* (Paddington), a permanent public artwork dedicated to Alan Turing. His collection *Out of Range* (Bloodaxe) includes the poem 'The Future' which Andrew Scott recorded for Culture Declares Emergency.

His opera librettos include *Between Worlds* (Barbican/ENO), composer Tansy Davies, director Deborah Warner;*Cave* (London Sinfonietta), composer Tansy Davies; and *Earth Song* (BBC Singers) composer Rachel Portman. His first screenplay, an adaptation of Raimond Gaita's *Romulus, My Father*, directed by Richard Roxburgh, won Best Film at the Australian Film Awards, and was shortlisted for Best Screenplay. Other theatre work includes: *To Reach the Clouds*, an adaptation of Philippe Petit's account of his walk between the Twin Towers (Nottingham Playhouse); *Success* for National Theatre Connections and *All The Angels* (Globe Theatre and Smock Alley Theatre).

Lynne Parker
Director

Lynne is Artistic Director and co-founder of Rough Magic.

Her productions for Rough Magic include: *Solar Bones* by Mike McCormack in an adaptation by Michael West, *Hecuba* by Marina Carr, *Cleft* by Fergal McElherron, *A Midsummer Night's Dream* by William Shakespeare with Kilkenny Arts Festival (Best Ensemble Irish Times Theatre Awards 2018), *Melt* by Shane Mac an Bhaird, *The Train, The House Keeper* (Irish Times Best New Play 2012*), Famished Castle, The Critic, Travesties, Peer Gynt, Phaedra, Don Carlos* (Irish Times Best Production 2007), *The Taming of the Shrew* (Best Production 2006), *Improbable Frequency* (Best Production, Best Director, 2004), *Copenhagen* (Best Production 2002), *Sodome, my love, Three days of Rain, The Sugar Wife, Northern Star, Spokesong, Pentecost* (Best Irish Production DTF 1995) *Hidden Charges, Down Onto Blue, Lady Windermere's Fan, Digging for Fire, Love and a Bottle* (Bank of Ireland/ Arts Show Award), *Danti-Dan, New Morning, I Can't Get Started, The Way of the World, The Country Wife, Decadence, Top Girls*.

Other Theatre includes – *Heavenly Bodies,* (Best Director, 2004), *The Sanctuary Lamp, Down the Line, The Trojan Women, The Doctor's Dilemma, Tartuffe, The Shape of Metal* (Abbey Theatre); *The Drawer Boy* (Abbey Theatre/ Galway Arts Festival); *Lovers*

(Druid); *Bernard Alba, Me and My Friend* (Charabanc); *Catchpenny Twist* (Tinderbox); *Bold Girls* (7:84 Scotland); *The Shadow of a Gunman* (Gate Theatre); *The Clearing* (Bush Theatre); *Playboy of the Western World, Silver Tassie* (Almeida Theatre); *Playhouse Creatures* (Old Vic); *Importance of Being Earnest* (West Yorkshire Playhouse); *Love Me?!* (Corn Exchange); *Comedy of Errors* (RSC); *Olga, Shimmer* (Traverse Theatre); *Dancing at Lughnasa,* (Teatrul National Bucharest), *Only the Lonely* (Birmingham Rep); *La Voix Humaine* (Opera Theatre Company); *A Streetcar Named Desire* (Opera Ireland); *The Drunkard, Benefactors* (B*spoke); *The Girl Who Forgot to Sing Badly* (The Ark/Theatre Lovett); *Macbeth* (Lyric Theatre Belfast); *The Cunning Little Vixen, Albert Herring* (RIAM). Most recently, Seamus Heaney's *Beowulf* (Tron Theatre, Glasgow) Stewart Parker's *Northern Star, The Provoked Wife* by John Vanbrugh, Gorky's *Children of the Sun* and Schnitzler's *la Ronde, The Merchant of Venice* (The Lir Academy).

She was an Associate Artist of Charabanc Theatre Company.

Lynne was awarded the Irish Times Special Tribute Award in 2008 and an Honorary Doctorate by Trinity College Dublin in 2010.

Hélène Montague
Musical Director

Helene Montague was born in Stockholm and moved to West Cork where she was educated at home with music as first subject. Both her parents danced with the Royal Swedish Ballet, and she studied dance and theatre from an early age. Moving to Dublin at age 16 she studied piano with Dorothy Stokes and composition with James Wilson. Her first Musical Direction was *The Rise and Fall of the City of Mahagonny* by Brecht/Weill for Trinity Players.

She is a founder member of Rough Magic Theatre Company and has worked frequently with them as an actor, musician, musical director and voice director. She has worked freelance as an actor and musician for theatre radio tv and film.

Opera Direction includes Verdi's *La Traviata* (Glasthule Opera); Mozart's *The Marriage of Figaro*; Samuel Barber's *A Hand of Bridge*; *Susannah's Secret* by Wolf Ferrari and Offenbach's *Route 66*

In 2019 she directed *Liberazione Di Ruggiero dall'isola Di Alcina* by Francesca Caccini staged in the Peacock Theatre and the Freemasons Hall for the Royal Irish Academy of Music.

In 2020 she directed the premiere of Kevin O'Connell's Opera *DreamCatchr* also for RIAM which has now been filmed for television, in collaboration with IADT (co-directed with John Comiskey)

Helene teaches in Inchicore College, and the Royal Irish Academy of Music

Cathal Synnott
Music and Recording Supervisor

Cathal Synnott studied at The Schola Cantorum at St Finian's College, Mullingar and subsequently at Trinity College, Dublin. Since then he has flourished as one of the theatre and music industry's most respected musical directors.

Highly acclaimed for his precision and musicianship, his work as musical director/musician includes: *Riverdance* (Broadway and International tours); *Blind Fiddler* (Lyric Theatre); *Improbable Frequency*, *The Train*(Rough Magic), *Sweeney Todd*, The *Threepenny Opera*, *Jaques Brel Is Alive And Well and Living In Paris*, *Assassins* and *A Christmas Carol* (Gate Theatre); *Flatpack* (Ulysses Opera Company); *Anglo The Musical* (Verdant Productions); *Into The Woods*, *The Cradle Will Rock* (The Lir); *Christmas With The Priests* (Irish Tour); *Once* (Landmark Productions); *Town Is Dead*, *Anna Karenina* (Abbey Theatre) and Camille O'Sullivan's *The Carny Dream* (Bound and Gagged).

Cathal is currently working as an Assistant Lecturer on the BA in Musical Theatre at MTU, Cork School of Music.

Sarah Jane Shiels
Set and Lighting Designer

SJ began designing lighting in Dublin Youth Theatre, completing a BA in Drama and Theatre Studies in 2006 and more recently a M.Sc in Interactive Digital Media in 2021 (Trinity College Dublin). Her work with Rough Magic began on the SEEDS programme from 2006 – 2008. From 2010 – 2017, she was founder and co-artistic director of WillFredd Theatre.

Recent lighting designs include *Conversations After Sex* (This Is Pop Baby); *Book of Names* (ANU); *The Veiled Ones* (Junk Ensemble); *Afterlove* (Stephanie Dufresne, Galway Dance Project, Galway Arts Festival); *The City is Never Finished* (Peter Power, Kilkenny Arts Festival); *I Walked into my Head* (Karan Casey, Kilkenny Arts Festival); *One Good Turn* (Abbey Theatre); *Day Crossing Farm* (Marie Brett, Cork Midsummers Festival); *Woman in the Machine* (Carlow Arts Festival); *Party Scene* (This is Pop Baby); *What Did I Miss?* (The Ark); *Sruth na Teanga* (Branar Téatar do Pháistí); *Hansel and Gretel* (Irish National Opera, Theatre Lovett, Abbey Theatre) and *A Very Old Man with Enormous Wings* (Collapsing Horse).

Sorcha Ni Fhloinn
Costume Designer

Since graduating with a BA in Drama and Theatre Studies from the Samuel Beckett Centre in Trinity College Dublin in 2015, Sorcha has worked extensively as a costume designer, maker and supervisor for theatre, film and music videos in Ireland and the UK. She is also a graduate of the Postgraduate Diploma in Theatre Costume course at the Royal Academy of Dramatic Art.

Previous design credits include: *Love + Information* (TUD Grangegorman); *Queenish* by Soulé (Diffusion Lab); *Close Quarters* (RADA Gielgud Theatre); *Requiem for the Truth* (Collapsing Horse); *Fierce Notions* (Smock Alley Theatre); *Talk To Me Like the Rain* (Bewley's Café Theatre); *Test Dummy* (Theatre Upstairs); *Gays Against The Free State!* (Smock Alley Theatre); *Hornet's Nest* (ANU Productions).

Fiona Sheil
Sound Designer

Fiona Sheil is a Sound designer and Composer. She graduated with a Masters in Experimental Sound from UCC in 2020. Fiona was nominated for The Hearsay Audio Prize 2021.

Collaborations with Catherine Young include *State of Exception*, *Ultima Thule*, *The Choreography Project*, *The river will still run to* the sea for Mind your step and *Welcoming the Stranger* as part of The Casement Project 2016.

Other design credits include *Glue* (Rough Magic); *No one see the video* directed by Samantha Cade; *Holy Mary* by Eoin Coilfer; *Madhouse* by Una McKevitt & PJ Gallagher (DFF/Abbey Theatre); *Anatomy of a Suicide* directed by Tom Creed and *CITY* by John McCarthy at the Everyman Theatre.
She was chosen for The Centre Stage project 2020/21, run by Theatre Forum, with La Escuela Pública de Formación Cultural (Spain), & Kultur i Väst (Sweden). Upcoming projects include Catherine Young's *Floating on a Dead Sea* as part of Dublin Dance Festival 2021 & Rough Magic's *All the Angels*.

Brian Doherty
George Frideric Handel

Theatre credits include *Hecuba*, *Pentecost*, *Improbable Frequency*, *Boomtown* (Rough Magic); *Common*, *Aristocrats* (National Theatre); *Antony and Cleopatra*, *Winter's Tale*, *Little Eagles*, *Macbeth*, *God in Ruins*, *The Drunks*, *Great Expectations* (RSC); *The Wake*, *Three Sisters*, *Down the Line*, *Translations*, *Tarry Flynn* (Abbey Theatre); *The Seagull*, *Sive*, *Famine* (Druid); *The Father*, *From Here To Eternity*, *Stones in his Pockets* (West End); *Tomcat* (Papatango); *Death of a Comedian* (Soho); *A Steady Rain* (Theatre Royal Bath); *Narratives* (Royal Court); *The Red

Iron, *Happy Birthday Dear Alice*, *The Crucible*, *Observe The Sons of Ulster Marching Towards the Somme*, *Talbot's Box* (Red Kettle); *STUDS* (Passion Machine) and *Evening Train* (Everyman).

Film and TV credits include: *Resistance*, *Trigonometry*, *Witless*, *Casualty*, *Raw*, *Pure Mule*, *Fair City*, *Glenroe*, *Dreamhorse*, *A Street Cat Named Bob*, *Perrier's Bounty* and *Garage*.

Ross Gaynor
Crazy Crow / Charles Burney/ Jennens / Cavendish

Ross is an actor and a writer from Dublin. He is a graduate of The Lir Academy and of University College Dublin, where he received the Ad Astra scholarship for Drama.

Theatre credits include: *The Valley of The Squinting Windows* (CityTheatre Dublin); *Bullfight on Third Avenue* (Bewleys Café Theatre); Mozart's *Der Schauspieldirektor* (Irish National Opera); *Mr.Burns: A Post-Electric Play* (Rough Magic: SEEDS); *The Train* (Rough Magic); his own one-man play *I AM A BIRD NOW* (Theatre Upstairs); *If We Can Get Through This (So Can You)* (Abbey Theatre/The 24Hour Plays: In Aid of DYT); *Dinner and A Show* (Gentle Giant Productions) and many other productions in The Lir.

Film and TV credits include: *Cave* (Banjoman Films), *Valhalla* (MGM/ Netflix), *Normal People* (BBC/

Element Pictures), *Blasts From the Past* (RTÉ/Firebrand), Bernard Dunne's *Mythical Heroes* (RTÉ/Firebrand), *Abilita – Rumori Dal Fondo* (Carboluce), *Resistance* (RTE), *The Comedian* (Banjoman Films) and *What Richard Did* (Element Pictures).

Rebecca O'Mara
Susannah Cibber

Theatre credits include: *Furniture* (Druid); *Describe the Night* (Hampstead); *Melt* (Rough Magic); *Private Lives* (Gate); *Helen and I* (Druid); *Othello* (Abbey); *Chekhov's First Play* (Dead Centre); *Wuthering Heights* (Gate); *Aristocrats* (Abbey); *The Vortex*; *Pride and Prejudice*; *Mrs Warren's Profession* and *Hay Fever* (Gate); *Moment* (Bush); *Danton's Death* (National); *The Yalta Game* (Gate, Sydney/Edinburgh International Festivals); *Far from the Madding Crowd* (ETT); *Deep Blue Sea* (Theatre Royal, Bath/Vaudeville); *Salt Meets Wound* (Theatre503).
Film work includes: *The Toxic Avenger*; *Herself*; *Jimmy's Hall*.

Television credits include: *Line of Duty*; *Bump*; *Red Rock*; *The History of Mr Polly* and *Doctors*.

Rebecca won the 2019 Irish Times Theatre Award for Best Actress in a Supporting Role.

Rebecca trained at the London Academy of Music and Dramatic Art.

Megan O'Neill
Soprano / Signora Avoglio

Megan O'Neill is a soprano from Killarney, County Kerry. She is currently studying with Prof. Mary Brennan and Dr Andrew Synnott. She completed the BMus Degree in Maynooth University in 2018 and graduated with a First Class-Honours Degree. In August 2020, she completed the Masters in Music Performance Degree at the Royal Irish Academy of Music, where she also received a First Class-Honours. She is currently in her second year of a Doctor in Music Performance Degree at the RIAM.

In 2019, Megan played the role of Mary-Braud in the Irish première of the opera *Banished* by British composer Stephen McNeff. Later in 2019, she played the role of Sirena in Francesca Caccini's opera *Alcina* at the Abbey Theatre, gaining her a feature in The Irish Times. In November 2020, she was awarded second prize in the Irené Sandford singing competition. Megan was a finalist in the prestigious Maura Dowdall Concerto Competition in March 2021, where she performed Handel's *Gloria in Excelsis Deo*. Megan was awarded The Dermot Troy Trophy in the Feis Ceoil 2021, where she sang 'Let the Bright Seraphim' from *Samson* by Handel and was also commended in The Dramatic Cup for her performance of 'O zittre nicht' from *Die Zauberflöte* and 'Les oiseaux dans la charmille' from *Les Contes d'Hoffmann*. She was also a finalist in The Gervase Elwes Memorial Cup.

She will soon been seen in the lead role of Jane in the world première of the film opera *DreamCatchr* by Kevin O'Connell, which will be released in 2022.

Ross Scanlon
Tenor

Ross Scanlon trained at the DIT Conservatory of Music and Drama where he was awarded the Michael McNamara Gold Medal of excellence in performance and at the Royal Academy of Music, London.

At the Royal Academy of Music Opera School his roles included Lurcanio *Ariodante,* Masino *La vera Costanza,* Monostatos *Die Zauberflöte* and Scaramuccio *Ariadne auf Naxos.*

Elsewhere, his roles have included Le Thérière *L'Enfant et les sortlièges* with the BBC Symphony Orchestra, Barbican, London, Hot Biscuit *Paul Bunyan* for Welsh National Opera, Irus *The Return of Ulysses* for Opera Collective Ireland, Male Chorus *The Rape of Lucretia* for Opera Collective Ireland, Ed *A Belfast Opera* for NI Opera, Bookkeeper *The Rise and Fall of the City of Mahagonny* for OTC, Dublin, Remendado *Carmen* for Lyric Opera, Dublin and Tamino *Die Zauberflöte* for Glasthule Opera.

Ross sings widely in concert, his engagements including *Alexander's Feast, Messiah* and *The Creation* with the RTÉ Concert Orchestra,

Messiah at the Halle Festival, Germany, at the Handel Music Festival, Dublin, and with the Irish Philharmonic Orchestra. Other oratorio's include Britten *Saint Nicolas,* Dvořák *Stabat Mater,* Handel's *Coronation Anthems,* Haydn *Die Jahreszeiten* and *Missa in Tempore Belli,* Mendelssohn *Elijah* and *St Paul,* Stainer *Crucifixion,* Mozart's *Vesperae Solemnes de Confessore* and *Coronation Mass,* Schubert's *Mass in B flat,* Jenkins *'The Armed Man – A Mass for Peace'* and Goodall *Eternal Light – A Requiem* (Irish Premiere).

Recent engagements include performing for HRH, Prince of Wales, with The Ulster Orchestra, Belfast, Irish Premiere of Howard Goodall's *Invictus: A Passion* with Bray and Wicklow Choral Societies, Bach *Magnificat* and Respighi *Lauda per la Nativtà del Signore* with Ancór Choir, Limerick.

Ross is a member of the Vocal Faculty at the American College, Dublin where he lectures on the Musical Theatre Course and is also an Examiner for the Royal Irish Academy of Music.

Owen Gilhooly-Miles

Baritone

Owen Gilhooly-Miles is a graduate of the Royal College of Music and National Opera Studio in London. He made his Royal Opera House debut singing the Fauré *Requiem* for The Royal Ballet and in 2007 represented Ireland at BBC Cardiff Singer of the World. He is also a Professor of Singing at the Royal Irish Academy of Music.

He has appeared in principal roles with Opera Ireland, Opera Theatre Company, English Touring Opera, Lyric Opera, Scottish Opera, Opera North and Buxton Festival Opera, The Opera Group and Musikverkstatt Wien. He has appeared in many productions for Wexford Festival Opera and Lismore Music Festival. In 2014 made his debut for The Royal Opera singing the role of Robert in the world premiere of Luke Bedford's *Through his Teeth*.

In concert he has appeared with the RTÉ National Symphony and Concert Orchestras, Irish Baroque Orchestra, Irish Chamber Orchestra, Ulster Orchestra, Bournemouth Symphony Orchestra and Tokyo Symphony Orchestras, the Royal Liverpool Philharmonic Orchestra and London Philharmonic Orchestras. He has performed at the BBC Prom in *HMS Pinafore* and Janáček's *Osud* with the BBC Symphony Orchestra, with whom he also performed in Judith Wier's *The Vanishing Bridegroom*.

ACKNOWLEDGEMENTS

Rough Magic would like to thank our Patrons, we could not do this work without your generous support.

Abirgreen Ltd, Desmond Barry, Ray and Mary Bates, Gordon Bell, Lillian Buchanan, Caroline Canning, Catherine Cashman Santoro, Alison Cowzer and Michael Carey, Donall Curtin, Elma Cusack, Ultan Dillon and Grazielly Noronha Muniz, William and Catherine Earley, Julian Erskine, John Fanning, Mary Finan, Anne Fogarty, Roy Foster, Kathryn Gilfillan, Michael Gleeson, Joseph Hasset, Timothy King, Hidden Peak Ltd, Aine MacCallion, Pat Mangan, R.J. McBratney, Denis and Elma McCullough, David Nolan, Cormac Ó Cuilleanáin, John O'Donnell, Sheila O'Donnell and John Tuomey, George and Margaret Parker, Ian Scott, Gerry Smyth, Gordon Snell and those who prefer to remain anonymous.

Special thanks to Brian Arkins; BA Steel; Barry Conway; Fransiska Detrez; Des Kenny; Kat Ennis; Ellen Murray; Noel Murphy and all at the Lir Academy

All the Angels

Nick Drake is a poet, playwright and screenwriter. *The Man in the White Suit* (Bloodaxe Books, 1999), won the Waterstone's/Forward Prize for Best First Collection. He was one of the Next Generation Poets chosen by the Poetry Book Society in 2004. *From the Word Go* (Bloodaxe Books 2008) was followed by *The Farewell Glacier* (Bloodaxe Books, 2012), a collection which grew out of a voyage in the Arctic. The poems were recorded for *High Arctic*, an installation by United Visual Artists at the National Maritime Museum. His long poem 'Message from the Unseen World' (2016) was commissioned for a permanent public artwork by UVA dedicated to Alan Turing located in Paddington. A new poetry collection, *Out of Range* (Bloodaxe, 2018) included 'The Future' which Andrew Scott recorded for Culture Declares Emergency. His opera librettos include *Between Worlds*, composer Tansy Davies, directed by Deborah Warner (ENO/Barbican 2015); *Cave*, composer Tansy Davies, directed by Lucy Bailey (London Sinfonietta/Royal Opera, 2018); and the poem for *Earth Song*, composer Rachel Portman (BBC Singers). Other theatre work includes *To Reach the Clouds* (Nottingham Playhouse), and *Success* (Faber) for NT Connections, at the Oliver Theatre and around the UK. He wrote the screenplay for *Romulus, My Father*, starring Eric Bana, which won Best Film at the Australian Film Institute Awards. www.nickfdrake.com

NICK DRAKE

All the Angels

Handel and the First Messiah

faber

First published in 2016
by Faber and Faber Limited
74–77 Great Russell Street
London WC1B 3DA

Typeset by Country Setting, Kingsdown, Kent CT4 8ES
Printed and bound in the UK by CPI Group (Ltd), Croydon CR0 4YY

A CIP record for this book
is available from the British Library

978-0-571-33714-9

4 6 8 10 9 7 5 3

To Claire Egan
soprano

Acknowledgements

My thanks to:

Jonathan Munby, who had the best ideas, and
transformed this play into a glorious production.

David Horovitch, Kelly Price and Sean Campion,
whose input enhanced the play no end, and whose
beautiful performances realised it beyond my dreams.

Dominic Dromgoole, for commissioning the play
in the first place.

Ruth Smith, for so kindly sharing her expert
knowledge of Handel and Jennens,
and for her insights and notes on drafts of the play.

Emma Rice, Tom King, Harry Nyland,
the staff and the stewards at the Wanamaker,
and Julia Kreitman, my agent.

Richard Luckett, for *Handel's Messiah: A Celebration*
(Gollancz) which set me on the path of this story.

John Dove, for many Christmas *Messiahs*.

Naomi Wallace, for a conversation about *Messiah*,
years ago.

Claire Egan, soprano, for so generously confiding
her knowledge of the arts and mysteries of singing.

All the Angels was first staged in this version in the Sam Wanamaker Playhouse at Shakespeare's Globe, London, on 6 December 2016. The cast, in order of appearance, was as follows:

Crazy Crow / Jennens / Cavendish Sean Campion
George Frideric Handel David Horovitch
Susannah Cibber Kelly Price
Ensemble Soprano / Signora Avoglio Lucy Peacock
Ensemble Mezzo-Soprano Saskia Strallen
Ensemble Tenor / Charles Burney Laurence Smith
Ensemble Bass Paul Kemble

Additional roles played by the company

MUSICIANS
Michael Haslam (*Musical Director / Harpsichord*), Jorge Jimenez (*Violin I*), Naomi Burrell (*Violin II*), Joanna Levine (*Cello*), Adrian Woodward (*Trumpet*)

SINGERS FROM THE SIXTEEN
Tom Castle, Nancy Cole, Camilla Harris, Rebekah Jones, Angus McPhee, Ben Vonberg-Clark, Daisy Walford, Jamie Wright

Director Jonathan Munby
Designer Mike Britton
Movement Director Imogen Knight
Assistant Director Martin Leonard
Costume Supervisor Sydney Florence

All the Angels was originally produced in 2015 by Dominic Dromgoole

All the Angels was revived at Smock Alley Theatre, Dublin, on 20 November 2021, produced by Rough Magic and Smock Alley Theatre. The cast and creative team were as follows:

George Frideric Handel Brian Doherty
Crazy Crow / Charles Burney / Jennens / Cavendish Ross Gaynor
Susannah Cibber Rebecca O'Mara
Soprano / Signora Avoglio Megan O'Neill
Tenor Ross Scanlan
Baritone Owen Gilhooly-Miles

Director Lynne Parker
Musical Director Helene Montague
Music and Recording Supervision Cathal Synnott
Set and Lighting Designer Sarah Jane Shiels
Costume Designer Sorcha Ní Fhloinn
Sound Designer Fiona Sheil
Hair and Make-up Val Sherlock
Assistant Director Dominic O'Brien

Characters

George Frideric Handel
fifty-seven, big, awkward, imposing,
dignified, grumpy, benevolent,
capable of titanic rages.
Wears a major wig

Susannah Cibber
twenties—early thirties,
tragic actress who sings

Crazy Crow
Irish, of indeterminate age

also plays

Charles Jennens, *librettist*
William Cavendish, *Lord Lieutenant of Ireland*
and other small parts

Charles Burney
teens

Singers / Actors
Soprano, Mezzo, Tenor, Bass

ALL THE ANGELS

Act One

The Chorus sing out with all their hearts:

Chorus
'Hallelujah, hallelujah, hallelujah, hallelujah,
hallelujah . . .'

> *Suddenly the trapdoor slams open, stopping the Chorus
> dead.*
> *A wild, dishevelled figure rises, festooned with
> instruments – a black case on his back, a horn around
> his neck, a trumpet in one hand, a violin and flute in the
> other.*

Crazy Crow (*Irish*) Halle-feckin'-lujah yourselves. If I say
this is the year of Our Lord one thousand seven hundred
and forty-two, and here I stand, in Dublin, fair city, *not* –
you'd better believe me. You see . . . Ireland has suffered
greatly, these last years. A cruel winter, followed by a
burning summer, and then another calamity of storms,
blizzards and frosts. Harvests devastated. Fish dead in the
lochs. The mill wheels frozen in their courses. Famine. Fever.
And no relief. They call it, the Year of Slaughter . . . They
call me Crazy Crow, but that is not my real name, which I
shall not tell you. And in case you're asking, I am *not drunk*,
or a wife-beater. This is a refined theatre, and I am of the
back street beyond the back street. So what am I doing in
here? Well, I'll tell you. Well, maybe you can guess. By day
I'm the musicians' porter. They make the beautiful music,
with these mad contraptions of hollow wood and tinkling
brass and elephant ivory and keening cat gut; but someone
has to do the lifting, the carrying, the sweating, the back-
breaking, zero-hours, no-contract no-pension, no-thankyou

labouring! The enchanted emerald isle may be full of sweet noises but someone round here has to do the fecking *work*! But Christ, they pay miserable peanuts. So I'll be off, soon, when the sun sinks and no moon rises, to my other, darker trade just next door – *down St Andrew's graveyard*. More of that anon. But listen: I will be part of this story. And I will play many parts in this story. Because even though I am of the back streets, and not of the musical wonder-world, this is my story too. I was there. Watching. Listening. Raging! And I saw him, with these glittering eyes. The Great Composer. Mr Handel. *And Crazy Crow has a bone to pick with him* . . . Believe me, don't believe me. We start before Dublin. It's winter. There's a man in a coach with a black portmanteau bag at his side. The roads have rattled his teeth all the way from London heading north. His head is full of shadows, he fears he's finished, he's been ill and has not fully recovered, despite the appearances he maintains, and his finances are what you might call – *catastrophic*. But now the sky has turned storm dark, the wind is blowing, and a hard rain is going to fall . . . On *Chester* . . .

Sounds of the storm, a great blowing wind . . .

SCENE TWO

The Golden Falcon Inn, Chester.
The Chorus sings.

Chorus

'And with his stripes we shall be healed –'

But the Bass makes a mistake.
Now, from the back of the theatre, Handel storms on to the stage wearing a large white wig, in a rage.

Handel HALT!

Silence.

This is nothing but a simple fugue! The instruments double the voices! What is so complicated about that? Again.

The Chorus Master has them begin again.
The Bass makes the same mistake.

HALT! I requested Choristers who could sing at sight! And that means at *first* sight!

Silence as Handel prowls like a titan among the Chorus.

I have written Coronation anthems for Kings. Funeral music for Queens. Oratorios and cantatas. Odes and masques. Church music in Latin, German and Italian. Canticles, concertos, concerti grossi, arias, chamber music, keyboard suites, trios, sonatas, serenatas and songs!

Crazy Crow And forty-two operas!

Handel Don't talk about the opera!

Silence.

I am my own industry. There is even a statue of me, in Vauxhall Gardens. I have now written a new work. An oratorio. You have that work before you. Why? Because although I should be in Dublin, rehearsing, the sea is in the sky, and the wind blows backwards and the cowardly packet boat refuses to sail, and so I am stuck for four *beschissene* days, in *beschissene* CHESTER!

He tries to control himself.

But I must make the best of it. Your choir master has lent you to me, and so you, God help me, are the first human voices to sing any of it. So we may be in a room above the *verficktem* Golden Falcon Inn, but you will please imagine you are in your Cathedral and it is Passion week, and God is listening. Do not disappoint me again.

Now the Chorus sings again:

Chorus

'And with his stripes we are healed . . .'

A Young Man (Charles Burney) creeps in to listen, enthralled . . .

SCENE THREE

The Golden Falcon Inn. Wind and rain blow on . . .
Handel removes his wig, and lowers his head into his hands, in despair.
Charles Burney enters bearing a dish of coffee in his trembling hands, and with anxiety and awe sets it before the great man. He waits as long as he dares. Then:

Burney (*nervous*) Sir . . .?

Handel The Lord giveth and the Lord taketh away. Blessed be the Lord –

Burney Amen –

Handel (*anger gathering*) He blows me back, again and again! *Why?* Failure after failure! Reverse upon reverse, does he think I have the patience of Job? And what can His divine purpose possibly be in keeping me prisoner in *Chester?*

Burney Chester's actually quite nice. There are the city walls, and the canals, and the Watch –

Handel If I were a tourist, boy, I would choose Florence or Rome –

Burney (*dreaming*) Oh Italy!

Handel (*sailing on*) – not *beschissene* Chester, where I am confronted by this River Dee, which is the muddiest and least musical water I have ever had the misery to wait upon!

He drinks all the coffee.

Burney More coffee?

Handel NO! Yes.

Charles Burney pours more coffee.
    The wind rattles the windows again. Handel laughs, bitterly.

Ha! Even the wind torments me.

Burney (*he knows*) But you write so much music for wind, sir. Flute, bassoon, haute-bois . . .

Beat.

Handel How do you know that?

Burney I'm music-mad, Sir.

Handel Oh God . . .

Burney I love the organ, as I know you do too, Sir. Mr Baker, the organist at the Cathedral, had a fit of gout, and needing an assistant he quickly taught me to play a chant before I even knew my gammut or the keys –

Handel And did you so?

Burney I did. I like to extemporise, and I'm also learning the violin, and French. Please, Sir, the Water Musick, tell me how it was?

Handel No, no . . . Leave me alone.

The look on Charles Burney's face makes him relent.

It was a summer night. A clear sky. A useful moon. I herded fifty musicians on to a barge. They performed the work, accompanying the King as the rising tide carried him towards Chelsea. The banks of the river were crowded, making a grand audience for a concert upon the water. The King disembarked at Chelsea, was entertained at a late supper, and then ordered the entire piece repeated, at three in the morning, under the moon and the stars, as he returned to Whitehall. He loved it. I returned to favour. Twenty-five years ago . . .

He looks glum.

Burney How's the favour going?

Handel So-so.

He slurps more coffee.

Burney Perhaps you could write something for the other elements?

Handel Oh, Earth Music, a brilliant idea –

Burney I was thinking – Fire, perhaps?

Handel says nothing, but makes a grudging little note in his notebook.

Handel You are not unintelligent.

Burney Tell that to my father –

Handel He does not approve of your music?

Burney He thinks it's a terrible idea.

Handel So did mine. He wanted me to become a lawyer.

Burney How ghastly!

Handel (*amused*) Are you not afraid of me?

Burney Oh yes, very much so! But I knew I must speak with you, if I could.

Handel You compose?

Burney I want to –

Handel Either you do or you don't. Start now.

Burney Yes. I wondered –

Handel No no no – I take no pupils.

Burney Of course, of course . . . But, Sir: what do you think of chromaticism?

Handel *What?*

Burney Everyone in Chester seems to hate it, but I like its effects; and I was thinking, surely, if discord is allowable, why could noise itself not be opposed to fixed sounds and harmonic proportion?

Handel shakes his head in amazement.

Handel Dear God. What is your name?

Burney Burney, Sir, Charles Burney.

Handel Well, Charles Burney, Sir, I don't hate chromaticism, indeed I use it myself, judiciously, but I do *hate* waiting.

Burney casts around for another subject to keep the conversation going.

Burney Sir, I have heard wonderful things of your operas, and I hope one day –

Handel The opera . . . is over.

Burney Oh. But . . . why?

Handel The last season. Failure. Disaster . . . *kaputt.*

Silence.

Burney It was the greatest moment of my life to hear that part of the new oratorio, in your presence . . . I thought it was *wonderful.* Music is everything to me, Sir. It is my life. You inspire me.

Beat.

Handel Take a seat, Mr Burney, Sir.

Handel reaches into the portmanteau and produces a score. Burney reads the title page.

Burney (*with awe*) *Messiah: an Oratorio* –

Handel To the glory of God.

He allows Burney to look through.

They say you can't fight the waves or change the wind and yet I find a man must continuously struggle to do those very things. I thought it would get easier. It doesn't.

Burney Only the music matters, Sir. God hears it.

Handel That is true, Mr Burney. Why don't you bring two glasses, and something stronger than coffee?

Burney Yes, Sir. At once, Sir.

He runs off. Handel watches him go. And he smiles.

Instrumental: 'Every Valley shall be Exalted'.

SCENE FOUR

Crazy Crow But hold on now, stop the clock, and wind back its pickpocket's hands! We're forgetting something. Or *someone*. We're going back now, to summertime, of last year, to Leicestershire. To Gopsall Hall. We enter the great house, uninvited. These people are rich, from iron and coal. We ascend the creaky stairs, and we find a passageway. We go along it, to a bedroom door, the bedroom of the only living son of that family. And when we open that door –

Crazy Crow transforms himself into Charles Jennens, with the manuscript of the libretto in his hand.

Jennens I must speak! I am Jennens. Charles Jennens. Of course, you all know the composer, but who remembers me? I am the librettist. I compiled the word book. I have chosen, organised and judiciously juxtaposed scriptural fragments from the Old and New Testament into a beautiful, glorious, dramatically coherent, magnificent new whole – (*Overcome.*) *Messiah!* The subject excels every other subject.

'God was manifested in the flesh, Justified by the spirit, seen of angels, preached among the gentiles, believed on in the world, received up into glory. in whom are hid all the treasures of wisdom and knowledge'

– i.e., the divine scheme –

Prophecy. Nativity. Passion. Resurrection. Ascension. *Messiah.*

He composes himself.

Mr Handel, whom I respectfully and yet privately call the Prodigious One, is my dearest friend. And yet, he has failed to visit me this last year. Alas. No doubt he is preoccupied in London, with his composing, and concerts and friends, or with gallivanting the continent. But I am stuck here, in *Leicestershire.* The very word strikes a blow to the heart, does it not? I have only my books and music for company, while my father downstairs drinks himself into a rage of oblivion, every night. We avoid each other. There is a reason, but I cannot speak of it.

No. Living at home is dreadful. Sometimes I feel I am becoming a ghost . . . But now there is this –

He holds out the manuscript, and kisses it.

Messiah. My finest work. Finished. Praise God. It has saved me, from despair. I shall send it to the Prodigious One. At once –

Jennens exits. The Chorus covers the scene change:

Chorus
'And the Glory of the Lord Shall be Revealed . . .'

SCENE FIVE

Dublin. A drawing room.
 At first, Handel is alone. He is exhausted. His hand shakes.
 Crazy Crow is now playing William Cavendish, 3rd Duke of Devonshire, Lord Lieutenant of Ireland, who sweeps in: charming, enthusiastic, and nervous to meet his hero.

Handel Ah, Lord Cavendish –

Cavendish Welcome at last to the Hibernian shore, my dear Sir! How do you find it?

Handel Closer than Iceland, is all I can say.

Cavendish Ah ha! You are settled in your apartments?

Handel If I can find them again, the city is all a shambles to me.

Cavendish Ireland is considered the apotheosis of Dullness. Granted, it is not sunny Italy, or Paris, or London; but you will find the Nobility and Gentry vastly excited by your arrival, and by the prospect of a season of your concertos, played by you, Sir –

Handel I confess I had never thought to come to Dublin. It never crossed my mind. But here I am, Sir, driven by the misfortune of pecuniary necessity – and by your kind invitation, of course –

Cavendish My dearest wish is to resolve you of such earthly anxieties. I love your music above all things –

Handel Above your wife!?

Cavendish (*confidential*) Sometimes!

Handel likes this.

Handel This is an unusual and perhaps perilous venture for me. Much is uncertain – the audience, the rewards, the potential for future performances –

Cavendish Let me reassure you, Dublin has an excellent musical life, and you are awaited as a god –

Handel I doubt it –

Cavendish You are a great artist. A treasure of the nation –

Handel Would that the treasure were in my bank account, Sir –

Cavendish I am aware of the, ah, *travails* that beset you in the last London opera season –

Handel holds up his hand at the word 'opera'.

Handel Never speak that word –

Cavendish – But I thought it surely a question of the audience, for in London their hearts are tangled and knotted by fanaticism, and corrupted by the critics –

Handel Gargoyles! Bickering little *arschkriecher kruppels*!

Cavendish Quite so! And yet here the Irish hearts are generously, indeed wildly, open to the new. Believe me, you will be welcomed. Your music gladdens us, Sir. It is necessary to us, for it touches our hearts.

Handel is moved by this. He turns aside, trying to master his welling emotions.

Are you well, Sir?

Handel Kindness. Why does it always surprise?

Cavendish Sir, I hope we may be friends.

Bowing, they embrace awkwardly.

Well. The Fishamble Street Musick Hall is ready for your inspection –

Handel (*every word baleful*) The Fishamble Street Musick Hall . . . Has it come to this?

Cavendish It is, Sir, the newest, finest and most accommodating purpose-built music hall in the city. Ideal, I assure you, for your season's purpose.

Handel Then I will start the task of assembling the season. Of composing the human element, with its inevitable disappointments. I shall draw from those musicians available here. I bring with me no galaxy of singers, so I hope the audience shall not be disappointed by the lack of stars – excepting Signora Avoglio, an excellent soprano, whom I have persuaded over, and who arrives soon by the yacht, which is absurdly expensive and for which I have had to pay from my own pocket! But there is one other thing – and I require your absolute confidence –

Cavendish Of course –

Handel I am considering the performance of a new work, an oratorio, in Easter week–

26

Cavendish A premiere, for Dublin! My heart beats faster –

Handel Dublin is an opportunity to try it out, before London. But I shall only do so if all the necessary elements are fully in place. It needs minimal musical forces only. But I absolutely require an excellent chorus, and I am told the Cathedral choirs are competent –

Cavendish Ah – well –

Handel What?

Cavendish It's complicated.

Handel I shall try to follow –

Cavendish There are two choirs in two Cathedrals in Dublin. The co-operation of both is required, because the choristers tend to sing in both choirs. And both Deans have to agree. Now one Dean is a notable lover of music, and I am sure will give his permission –

Handel But the other?

Cavendish Dr Swift –

Handel The author obsessed with the story about the little people with the unpronounceable name? Why, they say he is quite mad –

Cavendish He is Dean of St Patrick's, dear oh dear. And alas, he is notoriously unmusical –

Handel Sir, I must have a chorus.

Cavendish Then I shall set about the necessary persuasions at once –

He's going . . .

Handel One last thing. The new work demands a second excellent soprano soloist. And Dublin is not well supplied . . .

Cavendish Ah well, you need to hear Susannah Cibber, she has lately arrived for the theatre season –

Handel I know Mrs Cibber. She is an *actress* . . .

Cavendish An actress who sings.

Handel You strike fear into my heart, sir.

Cavendish She strikes joy into the hearts of all who listen.

Handel You make a fine advocate for Mrs Cibber's talents. But it would be impossible, alas. I write for highly trained professional singers. Not singing actresses.

Cavendish You should hear her, Sir.

He exits.

SCENE SIX

The Smock Alley Theatre.
Susannah Cibber on stage sings Thomas Arne's setting of Shakespeare.

Susannah
Come away, come away, death,
  And in sad cypress let me be laid.
Fly away, fly away, breath;
  I am slain by a fair cruel maid.
My shroud of white, stuck all with yew,
    O, prepare it!
My part of death, no one so true
    Did share it.

Not a flower, not a flower sweet,
  On my black coffin let there be strown.
Not a friend, not a friend greet
  My poor corpse, where my bones shall be thrown.
A thousand thousand sighs to save,
      Lay me, O, where
Sad true lover never find my grave,
      To weep there!

Handel sits to the side, listening intently. He doesn't
like the song, or Susannah's theatricalisation of it; but
he is surprised and moved by the authentic
melancholy beauty of her voice.
  Instrumental music covers the scene change.

SCENE SEVEN

Smock Alley Theatre dressing room.
  Susannah at a dressing table, brushing her hair. Handel
knocks on the door.

Handel Madam. I am –

Susannah I know who you are. Everyone knows who
you are –

Handel I want to talk to you about your voice . . .

Susannah Oh. You disliked it.

Handel Yes, technically. Musically –

Susannah I await your judgement.

Handel – I heard something.

Susannah Something you liked?

Handel Perhaps . . .

Beat. She extends her hand, he kisses it. Gallantry, and instant connection, but they are also sussing each other out.

Susannah How serendipitous we both find ourselves in Dublin.

Handel Ach! London . . .

Susannah Don't. I'm escaping –

Handel From what?

Susannah Surely you have heard?

Handel No one tells me anything. They think I'm too grand for gossip.

Susannah I used to love gossip – until I became its subject . . . You have heard?

Handel We shall never speak of it.

Susannah Are we then to speak of other things?

Handel I am going to teach you to sing –

Susannah is shocked.

Susannah Oh?

Handel I seek to cast a new work –

Susannah A new opera?

Handel No. An oratorio.

Susannah is disappointed.

Susannah That is impossible, for me, alas –

Handel Why?

Susannah Because – I am already engaged to the season upon the stage –

Handel No matter.

Susannah They work me hard. There is no time. The management would never release me, so I'm honoured, very much so, but –

Handel What roles do you play?

Susannah In *The Conscious Lovers* I am Indiana, beautiful and defenceless. I trust in the sincerity of a man who loves me, even though he is forced to appear duplicitous. In *Venice Preserv'd* I am Belvidera –

Handel Another innocent, whose trust leads to a madness of conspiracy and corruption from which only death can release you.

Susannah Alas.

Handel You toil with success in these absurd theatrical 'entertainments'. One must always work, no matter what – that I understand, and it is noble –

Susannah Actually, it is necessary –

Handel The matter is superficial, the music – apologies to Mr Arne – is mere popular stuff, your technique is not at all assured, ornaments, diction, time all doubtful, and yet – I believed you. You moved me. How? How did you do that?

Susannah Well, I suppose I –

Handel You drew upon your personal predicament and the emotions it engenders. Usually, when I am dragged to the theatre I see mannerisms, attitudes and untruths. It is a ridiculous business. But this was different. At moments . . . I heard something else.

Susannah What? What did you hear?

Handel A sorrow beyond your own sorrow. I want that sorrow. I want to put it to a greater work; to sing to God.

'He was despised, rejected of men, a man of sorrows, and acquainted with grief' – Isaiah, 53:3.

If one were to replace 'He' with 'She', does it not speak equally to woman?

Susannah Is that not blasphemous?

Handel Why should it be?

Susannah I am afraid . . .

Handel Fear goes instantly to the throat.

Susannah Yes –

Handel It goes to this –

He almost, but not quite, touches her throat –

This part of you that is as a bird, that is a wonder, that sings to the world and might perhaps yet sing to the Almighty himself . . .

She is entranced. It is intimate.

Susannah The Almighty? Why would the Almighty listen to me, of all people?

Handel Because he loves music. He made the world of it. Divine harmony. But above all he loves to hear us mortals sing our sorrows, and our joys, and our exultations. Human speech is but a whisper. But he delights to hear us sing. And then, all is forgiven . . .

They are close.

Susannah (*thrilled*) You terrify me, Sir.

Handel Fear demands courage. Nature loves courage. I shall help you and you will be wonderful. We begin tomorrow. And by the time Signora Avoglio arrives –

Susannah Who?

Handel My soprano. She is due here soon – to sing in my concert season –

Susannah Oh! An Italian . . . No doubt she is highly trained, greatly experienced, of immaculate technique and exquisitely beautiful.

Handel She is a most excellent professional.

Susannah But then – who am I to set beside her?

Handel You require flattery?

Susannah I seek to protect myself. I am clearly no match for her. Why do you not cast one of your great stars from the firmament of the opera world? Signora Cuzzoni, Signora Bordone?

Handel Those are fine singers, but of notoriously rivalrous temperament –

Susannah But they would never come to a place like Dublin, would they? And even if they did, at what ruinous price? Is that not the only reason you would consider a lowly creature, a theatre actress with a scandalous reputation, for your sacred oratorio?

Handel Do not diminish yourself. Those singers are highly trained, but for that very reason they have lost something essential. I need what they do not have, but you conspicuously do. I am asking you. Give me your voice and your time, and in a matter of two months I will turn you into a singer far greater than those perfected stars . . .

She stares at him.

Or refuse me . . . And I bid you farewell –

He prepares to depart.

33

Susannah How much of the music might be mine, and how much hers?

Handel I shall entrust a generous share of the singing to you. Is that good enough?

Instrumental and Bass: 'For Behold Darkness Shall Cover the Earth' . . .

SCENE EIGHT

Crazy Crow, no musical instruments this time, but instead a body in a shroud, which he drags out of the trap, as from a grave.

Crazy Crow Let me reveal to you the true glory of Dublin by night. Vice and violence and speculation worse than Nineveh city. If you go down Blind Quay, down the Piazzas, or Madden's in Smock Alley, down the hazard tables, at Reilly's or the Ben Jonson Head – watch out for Mendoza and his gang, they run false dice, and in the dark cellar are skeletons of victims who couldn't pay the proprietors of Hell. Be warned. As for me, when the night rises, but not the moon, I'm away to work, down St Andrew's graveyard. You see: I'm a resurrectionist. A body-snatcher, but a moral one. Now me, I don't kill. I merely survive off the dead, and they don't complain. Dublin surgeons at the College aren't bothered at all where they get their stiffs. All they want's a steady supply so they can slice 'em up on their anatomy tables with their great sharp knife blades to prove we're nothing but gristle and bone. What did that mad librettist fella say earlier? Prophecy. Nativity. Passion. Resurrection. Ascension. Messiah. Feck that! What about *me*? I'm the original man of sorrows! I'm the drink-meself-under-the-table feckin' resurrection

fella! I always bounce back – and as Death said to me
when I was a little boy – I saw him, standing in the room,
as close as I am now to you – *I'll see yous later* . . .

Chorus
   'Oh thou that tellest good tidings to Zion, good
   tidings to Jerusalem, arise, say unto the cities
   of Judah, behold, behold the glory of the Lord is
   risen upon thee . . .'

SCENE NINE

Fishamble Street Musick Hall.
   *Handel sets up a music stand, nervous in anticipation
of Susannah's arrival.*
   *As soon as he hears her approach, he sets himself in
an attitude of preoccupation, working on the score,
apparently deep in thought.*

   Susannah enters, nervous.

Susannah Good morning.

Handel Good morning, Mrs Cibber.

Susannah How are you?

Handel Fine. Very well . . .

   He continues to work.

Susannah (*taking her coat off*) Should I . . .?

Handel Yes . . .

   She puts down her things on a chair.
     She has a newspaper in her hand.

What do you have there?

She offers the newspaper:

'Her looks inform the trembling strings
And raise the passion, when she sings
The wanton Graces hover round
Perch on her lips, and tune the sound
Oh wondrous girl! How small a space
Includes the gift of human race!'

Who wrote this *scheisse*? Unsigned! The coward –

Susannah It's nice to be praised.

Handel Praise is as passing as censure, as you should know by now. What matters is the work – so, to work. Have you prepared the music which I sent you?

Susannah prepares herself and sings

Susannah
'But who may abide the day of his coming
And who shall stand when he appeareth . . .'

Handel HALT!

Susannah What?

Handel Where to begin –? Your disposition, the confounding of the vowels, the fatigue of the breath, the grimaces and tricks – what has happened?

Susannah I think I shall go –

Handel (*thunders*) I think you shall not!

She hesitates, obeys. He masters himself.

Where does the voice come from?

Susannah From the heart. And the throat –

Handel But what supports it? The body –

He bangs her about her body – which offends her.
– which creates the breath, not forcing it, not pushing it,
but . . . *creating* it and uniting it with the head –

Susannah I see . . .

Handel But where does it start?

Susannah Well . . .

She proposes her bosom –

Handel No! Deeper!

She proposes her belly –

No no no! In the *fanny*!

Susannah (*shocked but amused*) I beg your pardon?

Handel You must be like a fisherman who casts his line
perfectly, down-down-down to the deepest place, the
dark mysterious pool of silence from which all rises . . .
then you wind her up, up, up, the shoulder blades widen,
the ribcage opens like a window, the bosom yields, the
throat flowers – you yawn like a lover waking on a May
morn –

They exaggeratedly, romantically yawn.

You trill your lips like a dove in love –

They trill their lips.

Your vowels grow long and lovely and lush like the hills
and vales of England –

She begins to apply this to the aria, sotto voce.
Until the head and the chest are united, the sound is
travelling now all the time, endlessly, like a spinning
wheel worked by an unseen foot, and the voice is sitting
upon the breath like a skylark hovering invisible in the
high air – and you *sing*!

It's as if he's lifted and cast her like a bird into the air.

Susannah
  'But who may abide the day of his coming,
  And who shall stand when he appeareth . . .'

*As she sings Handel steps slowly back, listening
intently. A quick nod to the musicians, who join . . .*
  *She deals with the long phrases, shaping them
eloquently, proving the point of the words, performing
them . . .*
  He's moved. He turns away. She comes to a stop.

You are displeased?

Handel It was – fine.

Susannah Fine?

Handel Ach . . . You are still an actress!

Susannah Well, I *am* an actress!

Handel And that is the problem! Does God want to hear
you acting? No!

Susannah So what does God want? Do you know?

Handel He wants to hear something from beyond you,
singing through you. He wants to hear himself singing
back to himself.

Susannah I am a singer, I am not a theologian . . .

Handel You must become the vessel! As pure as water!
The instrument so pure that all else is silent, leaving only
the music as the sole force of expression. No hands! No
emoting!

Susannah But that is theatrical, it is poetical –

Handel It is ridiculous! I am dedicating your voice to the
service of God, so for God's sake stand still! If I could

38

stick you in a barrel and fill it with sand, and keep you there, so you are just a head and a mouth, open, singing . . .

Susannah You would, wouldn't you?

Handel (*close*) Oh yes. Believe me, I am Beelzebub when I do not get what I want.

Susannah But I do not know what that is.

Handel I want the truth. Nothing less.

Silence.

Susannah (*sudden tears*) This is too hard.

She hurries off, distressed.
    He calls after her:

Handel Mrs Cibber!

But she has gone.

Damnation.

There's a knock on the door. Cavendish enters.

Cavendish Is all well?

Handel Why do you ask?

Cavendish It's only there appeared to be – possibly? – tears? In Mrs Cibber's eyes? As she hurried past me, just now?

Handel I wish I could say it was because she was so greatly moved by the progress we have accomplished. However, as I foretold, it turns out her lack of technique is insurmountable.

Cavendish Alas. But then –

Handel *What?*

Cavendish Who else?

Handel There is no one else. Therefore, there will be no *Messiah*.

Cavendish Oh dear. I see. And yet . . .

Handel And yet *what*?

Cavendish Perhaps Mrs Cibber deserves – as do we all, God knows – a second chance? It cannot be easy for her. She is alone here, separated from her child – a daughter, of two years, Molly, I believe –

Handel I despise persuasions of sentiment, Sir.

Cavendish I speak merely of facts, and of the potential of kindness. She has just begun.

Handel Are you saying I should not cut off my nose to be revenged upon my face?

Cavendish Oh no. I would never say that. But the world would be poorer without *Messiah*.

Handel And I would be poorer still for a disastrous *Messiah*. What news?

Cavendish (*nervous*) Well, Sir, leaving Mrs Cibber for the moment –

Handel Speak!

Cavendish The Dean of Christ Church, Dr Cobbe, proclaims himself your greatest admirer. But –

Handel But?

Cavendish He confessed himself *deeply* concerned by the conundrum of the holy words being sung in a mere musick hall in holy week – but wonders what might the solution be –

Handel growls.

Handel And the Unmusical Dean?

Cavendish Dr Swift, despite his entrenched opposition to all things musical, was indeed persuaded by a clever subterfuge of his Sub-Dean's – also an undying admirer of yours – to sign the permission – which he did . . .

Handel Good –

Cavendish And we thought all was well . . .

Handel *But?*

Cavendish He then alas discovered the deception –

*He offers Handel a letter which Handel reads.
A terrible silence. Then he barks in rage:*

Handel The *ficken schweinhund*! Take me to him *at once*!

Cavendish That really won't help. You see he is quite mad. Doolalley. Fallen into a deep melancholy. Taken a wrong turn in his brain . . .

Handel (*furious*) Here is what you shall do. You shall return to these pious authorities and inform them that my *Messiah* is no trifling opera, of love and other foolishness, NO. The words are the holy words, and the music is dedicated to God. Tell them its purpose, in Easter week above all, is to remind the people on their knees, of their sorrow, their faith, and the glory of the Lord –

Cavendish Oh yes, that's rather good –

He makes a note.

Handel And if that is to be in a musick hall, then so be it. Tell them furthermore, that all the proceeds shall be given to charity. I have seen constellations of fine mansions in this city, and yet I am daily struck by poverty for which words themselves are beggared for belief. That should salve their sanctimonious consciences. Go –

Cavendish Yes. Of course.

He goes. He comes back.

But if Dr Swift continues to oppose?

Handel rages.

Handel *Gott im Himmel!* Must I do everything myself?!
Dean Swift, as I warned you, is deranged. Insanity has
inflicted its horrors upon him. His colleagues must for
pity's sake have him declared incapable. *Do it.* I will
have my chorus, or there will be no *Messiah* in Dublin.

Cavendish Does that mean, Mrs Cibber . . . ?

Handel (*furious*) *Go!*

Cavendish exits.
  Handel raises his fists to the heavens

(*Yelling.*) WHY DO YOU MAKE EVERYTHING SO . . .

He manages not to swear, just.

. . . DIFFICULT!

*He kicks away his chair in his rage. He stays in the
space, as Crazy Crow observes him.*

Chorus
'Surely He hath born our griefs, and carried our
sorrows . . .'

SCENE TEN

The Fishamble Street Musick Hall.

Crazy Crow sets up a single music stand.

Crazy Crow I've heard them all, the gentlemen
musicians who gather here, so well dressed, so bowing

42

and scraping, and then yanking and puffing away on their instruments, mewing like cats with mutual appreciation of the so-called music – and it meant nothing at all.

Susannah enters, placing her music on the stand.

But then, I heard something else. Mr Handel. His music. And then, one evening, I heard something else again. And there she was with her fair skin and the gilded stream of her hair, and her eyes of uninterrupted sorrow. Her beautiful hands were empty. No violin. No trumpet. No lute. She just opened her mouth . . . And I was drawn, like a moth, to a flame . . .

Susannah begins her warm-up, while testing out the acoustics of the performance space.
Crazy Crow watches her intently, from the shadows.
Now Susannah begins to practise in earnest.

Susannah
'For He is Like a Refiner's Fire
And who shall stand when he appeareth –'

She repeats the phrase, really working at her technique, as taught by Handel. She tries to sing without affect: simplicity, grace, openness, posture, communication of the force of the words, clarity of vowels, finding the place for the breath . . .
But it's very difficult. Frustrating . . .
Crazy Crow in the shadows circles her, utterly compelled by her voice and appearance.
She hears something. She stops.

Is someone there? Sir? Master?

Silence. Crazy Crow remains in the shadows, invisible to her.

43

You are teasing me, but enough now, Sir –

Nothing.

If someone is there, you must show yourself!

Crazy Crow Who the feck do you think you are, little girl?

It's an accusing voice out of the darkness.
Susannah is frightened –

Susannah I am –

Crazy Crow Nothing but a silly singing bird –

Susannah *Who are you?*

Crazy Crow Well, now, that is the question . . .

He is about to reveal himself. But then:
Handel enters. Crazy Crow melts away.

Handel Mrs Cibber –

She's really frightened:

Susannah Oh, thank the Lord. I thought –

Handel What?

Susannah tries to recover herself.

Susannah Nothing.

Handel Are you quite well?

Susannah Quite well. Thank you.

Beat.

Handel Our previous lesson –

Susannah I was –

Handel Yes. And I was –

44

Susannah Yes. You were.

Handel Well well. Here we are, and time is dripping away. So please – the aria I sent to you –

She is about to sing, but hesitates, nervous.

Susannah I have been practising it. But the runs are difficult – to swell them by degrees, and yet to make the words understood, to sustain the velocity and yet show no fatigue in the breath . . .

Handel So, you understand what you must do to acquire command. Please –

Susannah
'For He is like a refiner's fire
And who shall stand when he appeareth –'

She makes an error, falters, stops. Upset.

Handel What is it now?

Susannah What you are asking – I want to be courageous, and bold, and yet I am full of fear . . . of failure . . .

Handel Mrs Cibber. You either do this, or you do not do this. The decision is yours, the decision is everything, and the decision must be made now. I will teach you all I know. But if you are truly desirous of perfection –

But now: another soprano voice (offstage) sails out of the blue, a heavenly, trained, technically perfect voice:

Soprano (*a section of the aria*)
'Rejoice, rejoice greatly, oh daughter of Zion . . .'

Susannah listens, aghast at the technical excellence.

Handel Signora Avoglio has arrived.

Susannah She certainly has.

Handel She requires my immediate attention. These divas, you know. Continue, please –

Handel, excited, goes.
Susannah is distressed.

Susannah I can do this. I *can* –

Then:

Crazy Crow Why did you have to draw me out of the shadows?

He reveals himself. And he's angry.

Susannah Who are you, Sir? Your name –

Crazy Crow Could you not leave me in peace?

Susannah You are mad. I shall call for help –

Crazy Crow Who do you people think you are? I do not give a farthing for all the music in the universe. Orpheus himself was an utter eejit, with his lute charming the living and the dead, and even the stones to life? A likely story, and they tore his head off for it. But what you and the old fella have done is worse. Crueller. By far.

Susannah What? What have I done?

But now –
Avoglio sings again.

Avoglio
'Rejoice, greatly . . .'

Crazy Crow Listen to her!

Avoglio
'O daughter of Zion . . .'

Crazy Crow Think you can match that?

Avoglio
'Shout, O daughter of Jerusalem . . .'

Crazy Crow She's something else, isn't she?

He pats her arm, and goes.

Susannah Oh shit.

Interval.

Act Two

SCENE ELEVEN

Fishamble Street Musick Hall.
   Crazy Crow intervenes jokily as the Chorus sings:

Choir
   'For unto us a Child is born . . . a Son is given . . .
   And the government shall be upon his shoulders . . .
   And his name shall be called –'

Crazy Crow What is he?

Choir
   'Wonderful!'

Crazy Crow What's his job?

Choir
   'Counsellor!'

Crazy Crow Who is he?

Choir
   'Almighty God!
   The Everlasting Father, the Prince of Peace!'

They corpse. Crazy Crow exits.
   Handel has entered unseen.

Handel HALT!

Now he strides in and paces before them, titanic. They fear him.

'And I heard as it were the voice of a great multitude, and as the voice of many waters, and the voice of mighty thunderings, saying, Hallelujah, for the Lord God reigneth Omnipotent' – Revelations 19:6.

48

Gentlemen and ladies of the gentlemen's chorus: I know who you are. I know you fear you are as nothing. Just voices. One of many. Well, that is true. You are not soloists. You are the crowd. But: that is not nothing. It is the chorus that drive the music forward. In this work you are necessary. Fundamental. You tell good tidings. You are a scornful and scoffing multitude. You break our hearts with grief. Sometimes you are like sheep gone astray! You are the people who walk in darkness but see a great Light. You reveal the Glory of the Lord. You are *all the angels*. What more do you want? I write for the soloists. But I write more for you. And if you give me your hearts, with a great openness, then you shall be satisfied.

Silence.

Since you have so well learned the first part, let us move forward.

He raises his baton, the musicians prepare, and all perform 'Since by Man came Death'.

Chorus
'Since by man came death, by man came also the resurrection of the dead –'

SCENE TWELVE

Fishamble Street Musick Hall.
The lights diminish, and Chorus go into the shadows.
Silence.
Handel is in a small penumbra of candlelight.
His hand is shaking. He tries to calm it, folds it away, and with a difficulty we have not noticed before, he gets down on his knees, and, bringing his shaking hands together, prays.

49

Then a door bangs, in the dark; alarmed, he turns.
Crazy Crow enters from the shadows, festooned with black instrument cases, so all we see is a scary silhouette, spooking Handel.

Handel (*fear*) Who's there?

Crazy Crow waits.

Have you come for me again? I am not ready! It is too soon –

Crazy Crow reveals his face.

Crazy Crow I am only the porter, Sir. Did I frighten you?

Handel tries to recover from his fright.

Handel Of course not. Go on out now.

But Crazy Crow has no intention of going.

Crazy Crow Do you believe the holy words? About the resurrection of the dead?

Handel You were listening.

Crazy Crow I was waiting.

Handel Of course I believe the words. Music magnifies and dignifies them.

Crazy Crow They say you could make a line like: 'Could I have a pound of sausages please?' sound magnificent and dignified.

Handel What is your question?

Crazy Crow Well, perhaps it's not a question, more a kind of *consideration* of my own brain. You see, you almost made me believe in it all – but I have seen the resurrection, and the life, and, with the best will in the world, there is no music in it at all. In truth, it stinks.

Handel You speak only of the body. Not the soul.

Crazy Crow Perhaps that is so, Sir. The soul is not my business. The soul is more in the churchy-luxury-touchy-feely side of things . . .

Handel We all possess souls. What we do with them is another matter.

Crazy Crow is not impressed by this. Handel prepares to go.

Crazy Crow Let me tell you a little story –

Handel I'm tired –

Crazy Crow (*ignoring him*) You see, my own heart, which I lost long ago as a young boy, when like a coin it slipped from my fingers and fell between the floorboards into the dark, must once have been capable of the finer feelings, but it now is as ugly as a stone. And I've listened for years now to these fellas torturing their instruments here, and it means nothing at all. But when I heard your music . . . it made me angry.

Handel (*curious*) Why would my music make you angry?

Crazy Crow Well, that is the question that is dementing me. Tormenting, in fact. Inside my head.

Handel Perhaps you did not like it. Or perhaps, behind anger is fear – or grief . . .

Crazy Crow Behind anger, is more anger. It goes on forever, like two mirrors set against each other. People like me, we can't afford sweet airs. Or redemptions. Or tickets.

Handel You have your music. Every human creature does. Our mothers sing to us and as children we are like the birds, who sing without thought.

Crazy Crow True. My mother sang – and I would delight to listen to her –

Handel Well, there you are –

Crazy Crow And then she dropped down dead when I was but a young boy. Something went awry in her lovely head, you see, and one moment she was talking and smiling, and the next . . .

Handel sighs.

Handel In the midst of life . . .

Crazy Crow (*angry*) Halle-feckin-lujah.

Beat.

Handel What songs did your mother sing to you?

Crazy Crow Ah, now you're asking –

Handel I am.

Crazy Crow Well, there was one, we used to sing, and we'd laugh and act it out –

Handel Go on –

Crazy Crow *Me?* No, not at all, that's all in the past, lost and gone.

Handel What a pity. I should pay to hear some good Irish music.

Crazy Crow Would you so? Well lemme see, perhaps there's an inkling in the back of the cupboard of me head . . .

Handel Is there indeed? So –

He sits down, waits.

Crazy Crow
  'As I was goin' over the far famed Kerry mountains,
  I met with Captain Farrell, and his money he was
      counting.
  I first produced me pistol and I then produced me
      rapier,
  Saying: "Stand and deliver, for the Devil he may take
      you!"'

  Musha rin du-rum do du-rum da,
  Whack fol de daddy-o,
  Whack fol de daddy-o,
  There's whiskey in the jar . . .

  Crazy Crow is hurt by the memory.

Handel A fine ballad with a memorable chorus. But
what were those strange words?

Crazy Crow 'Whack fol de daddy-o –'

Handel (*noting in his book*) 'Whack fol de daddy-o . . .'

Crazy Crow What are you writing down there?

Handel The tune and the words. I might put them to use
one day. I like street cries.

Crazy Crow You are the first man ever to pay me for a
song.

Handel We must all be paid for our work. Especially
musicians. Otherwise, how do we live?

Crazy Crow Well, I will not tell you how.

Handel A man must defend his secrets. One thing is
clear, however. Your heart is not a stone.

  With that he goes, giving Crazy Crow a coin.

Now, out of the dark, comes the Chorus again singing to Crazy Crow. He doesn't like it.

Chorus

'Since by man came death, by man came also the resurrection of the dead . . .'

Crazy Crow Shut it! Shut it!

They continue . . .
He exits.

Chorus

'For as in Adam all die, even so in Christ shall all be made alive . . .'

SCENE THIRTEEN

Fishamble Street Musick Hall
A cold March morning.
Handel waits, impatient, anxious, pacing. Checks his watch . . .
Finally he hears Susannah, off, and hurriedly arranges himself in a pose of nonchalance, behind the newspaper.
Susannah enters hastily, taking off coat, gloves. She looks hungover and ill.

Susannah How dismally cold it is –

She blows her nose.

I fear I am unwell. Last night I was feverish. My head was ablaze, and I was shivering, but still, I went on, and they tell me I excelled myself.

She waits for his reaction. None comes.

And, after the show I had so many visitors it was impossible to get away. Even Mrs Kitty Clive, my rival, came to say goodbye and to wish me good luck, before she left for London . . . She was so gracious for one so very famous.

Handel noisily shakes out his paper, and continues to read.

And then a remarkable Hungarian, Mr Charles, dropped by, he plays the clarino, the horn, the hautbois d'amour, and the shalamo –

Handel finally slams down the paper.

Handel I don't give a *scheize* about the shalomo –

Susannah No?

Handel But my dear Mrs Cibber, if you arrive late one more time, cold or no cold, I shall pick you up and throw you out of the window. Do I make myself clear.

Susannah As glass.

Handel For God's sake! We have a week. Perfection of the voice is a painful acquisition, and it will never be achieved, let alone in time for the performance, if you go gallivanting about Dublin by night flirting with shalamo players!

Susannah I shall do as I please!

Handel Then you will never be a great singer. Never.

Susannah You are too harsh, Sir –

Handel I am truthful!

Beat.

Susannah You seem dismayed by something . . .

Handel I am dismayed by you!

Susannah And I by you!

Handel What do you want, Mrs Cibber? In your heart?

Susannah I want to be a great singer –

Handel How many other singers are out there? A sea of them! All drowning. Because they overdo it; they bark, or whisper, or sing as if they are thinking of something else, or they languish or hurry, or sing through their teeth, or sing as if laughing, or as if crying, or hissing, or they hallow or bellow and puff themselves up and torment the notes into ridiculous ecstasies and screams upon the highest notes. And they all think themselves the most talented parrots of perfection. You have something they will never have; a gift of nature. But you are too easily satisfied to aspire to the first rank. If you are truly desirous of perfection, you must work, every day, from dawn, for three hours at least, without fail. It will agonise you, and you will despair. But the beauty when it comes will amaze you.

They are very close.

Or, go off, enjoy yourself, stay up late, and be stuck forever singing ditties and fancies and songs your mother taught you. But that is not good enough, is it, Mrs Cibber?

Beat.

Susannah I have been working. Every morning. From dawn. For three hours. And more.

Handel But?

Susannah 'Not the best, and 'tis not the best, then 'tis nothing . . .' That is what they said of my singing . . .

Handel Ach –

Susannah It's true –

Handel You're feeling sorry for yourself –

56

Susannah I'm going to be found out! Signora Avoglio –

Handel There we have it –

Susannah Signora Avoglio will know within a heartbeat that I am a fake –

Handel Signora Avoglio has been a professional singer since she was fourteen, and very excellent she is –

Susannah (*unravelling*) Mrs Cibber, the scandalous actress singing the holy words? The audience will be taken ill with laughter! I shall be hooted out of Dublin, my career has already fallen apart once, and I cannot see how I will put it together again if this fails.

Handel bellows in frustration:

Handel Stop it! Stop talking! You are a great actress. You know what to do. Grasp your fear. Seize the moment. Sing your truth. Now. With me . . . I know you can do it.

Susannah Do you?

Handel Yes! 'He was despised . . .'

Susannah No, please, not today . . .

Handel The words. Let us start with the words. Speak them to me. *Plainly* . . .

Susannah
　'He was despised. Despised and rejected. Rejected of men. A man of sorrows and acquainted with grief . . .'

Handel Do those words speak to you?

Susannah Of course. I too have been despised. And rejected . . .

Handel By whom?

Susannah You said we would never speak of this.

Handel Tell me.

Susannah My husband. At first he stole my jewels, my gowns and my money to pay the madness of his debts.

Handel And then?

Susannah Then, when that money was gone, and the debts greater than ever, he connived to have me seduced by one of his creditors . . . William.

Handel Difficult?

Susannah My husband was cruel. He drank, frequented prostitutes, lied, cheated, betrayed me, repeatedly, blamed me for his failures, and then finally bargained my body. So yes, very . . .

Handel And so what happened?

Susannah William and I fell in love. Truly. He was quiet, and kind, and sincere. And yes, married. And my appalling husband was complaisance personified. He called him 'Mr Benefit'. That is, until we requested a separation. Oh, he didn't like that one bit. He took his revenge. At a tryst, in tawdry lodgings where we thought we were safe, and private, he had us spied upon, through a hole in the wainscot. The creature took copious notes of our . . . private intimacies. And then he sued William. There was a trial, it was all made scandalously public, including our positions and privacies and passions . . . as if we were no better than performing animals. All London was delighted. Susannah Cibber, the chaste actress, pilloried in disgusting cartoons and vile verses! The judge awarded him only the most paltry sum in compensation. But my reputation and my career were ruined. For who would employ me upon the stage now? And, I was with child, by William. I had lost two children before. But Molly lived, and she is my joy. But with that, my fall from society was complete. It sounds like the plot of one of my melodramas, I know. But the humiliation was all too real.

Handel So what do we do with such pain? We turn it into something else. You know this. So I want you to sing now, but replace the male pronoun with the female. Remember your pride, your dignity, remember you are not the sinner. Prove to me the point of the phrases. Tell me the story of your heart. Sing your deepest truth, and then the words will move us by their beautiful necessity.

She sings the aria, according to his instructions:

Susannah
'She was despised. Despised and rejected. Rejected of men. A woman of sorrows and acquainted with grief.'

She discovers a new emotional depth. He is moved. But hides it:

Handel You see. Getting there.

He prepares to go.

Susannah (*surprised*) You're going?

Handel So please, work on this, especially. But in the performance, think *She*, but sing *He*. Otherwise the ladies might all rebel against their perfidious husbands . . .

He is about to hurry off.

Susannah And you? Do you have pain?

Handel (*caught out*) Of course.

Susannah And what do you do with your pain?

Handel You have just sung it, Mrs Cibber.

He goes, leaving her amazed.

Chorus

'Let all the Angels of God worship Him . . .'

SCENE FOURTEEN

Gopsall Hall.
Jennens flourishes a letter in fury.

Jennens *Dublin?!* How *could* he? Of course the premiere
must be *London*! Oh, it is a calamity beyond bearing,
and to add insult to grave injury, he dares invite me to
cross the Irish Sea, to attend! *The Irish Sea?* Has he lost
his *mind*? Believe me, I would prevent him if I could!

Messiah of all my works matters, it deeply matters.
Why? Because there is such doubt and trouble in religion
in our time. Many now reject the intervention of God in
human affairs, they deny revelation, as if God merely
created everything, and then disappeared; and what do
they replace Him with? Human reason! Hilarious. Can
reason comfort grief? Can reason console misfortune?
Perhaps you do not greatly care about such matters. But
I do. And I shall tell you why. My own beloved brother,
Robert, died by his own hand, from the despair of
doubt. So badly, that he cut his own throat, and then
jumped from his window . . .

He is suddenly overcome.

What will become of his soul? How will he find salvation?
It is he who is the ghost, for ever walking the purgatory
of this sad house.

He breaks down, then composes himself.

Messiah is not just quotations from the Bible. It is my
meditation upon the supreme benevolent Goodness of
God. And that is why it begins as it does.

60

Comfort ye. Comfort ye . . .

Beat.

But I am not comforted.

Instrumental and Tenor;

Tenor
'Comfort ye. Comfort ye my people! Saith your God . . .
Speak ye comfortably to Jerusalem, and cry unto her
that her warfare, is accomplished, that her iniquity is
pardon'd –'

SCENE FIFTEEN

Fishamble Street Musick Hall.
*This time Susannah is waiting for Handel. She paces
the room, nervous; now she is like the lover waiting.*
*He enters at speed, brandishing a sheaf of manuscript
at her. She takes them as if they were flowers –*

Handel I have transposed something else from the
soprano for you –

Susannah Oh! Thank you . . .

Handel I decided the run of soprano recitative was too
much –

Susannah Well, Signora Avoglio does have it *all* from
'There were Shepherds abiding in the Field', through
'And Suddenly there was with the angel a multitude' . . .
Indeed, all the way through to 'Rejoice Greatly' . . .

Handel You have evidently studied her parts as well as
your own –

Susannah (*reading the manuscript*)
'He shall feed his flock like a shepherd' –

Handel No longer in B flat major but in F major – so now you also have a share in the shepherds, the fields and the flocks . . . although if you do not take to it, I might yet reconceive it as a duet for you and Signiora Avoglio.

Susannah Oh no!

Handel Or better yet, for a castrato . . .

Susannah I see you're teasing me –

He almost smiles.

Handel As long as you are happy.

Susannah Very. Perhaps you are gaining confidence in me . . .

Handel Perhaps that is so, Mrs Cibber.

She approaches him.

Susannah Would you be so kind as to call me Susannah?

Handel Mrs Cibber –

Susannah Don't worry. I shall always call you Master – you drive me to tears of despair, and yet I admire you with all my heart . . .

Handel (*avoiding*) We are striving for perfection, and so there is no room for sentimentality –

Susannah Or for sentiment?

Handel My dear –

Susannah Susannah –

Handel Susannah –

Susannah Forgive me, but you seem very – alone . . .

Handel Good God, woman –

Susannah They all say it is because the opera in London failed, and you feel betrayed . . .

Handel They do, do 'they'.

Susannah But I think that is not the answer.

Handel Perhaps you are too perspicacious for your own good.

Susannah You have no love to share your heart?

He is shocked.

Handel You are too forward.

Susannah I know.

Handel Just because you are in the enchantment of a new love does not mean such things are necessary or even given to all of us.

Susannah Love finds us all, whether we wish it or no. Whether we dare speak it, or no –

Handel What utter nonsense.

Susannah All I am saying is: I wish for you the warm glow of love. The intimacy, and the ease of it.

Handel Perhaps my heart is too narrow and cold for the warm glow of which you so eloquently speak –

Susannah I think it is a very great heart. Everything you write sings of love . . . and the sorrow of its loss . . .

Handel Then so does all music –

Susannah Have you lost love?

Handel Who has not, madam.

Susannah I do not mean to offend you. I only wish to –

Handel What? Humiliate me? Draw back the curtains

upon the secret history of my innermost, hidden, and as it seems, failed self? What for?

Susannah When I am in William's arms, I feel at home, at last. All I am trying to say is that I wish the same for you – no matter the *nature* of the arms . . .

Beat. He is speechless.

You speak to me of truth, nothing but the truth, but you yield none of yourself.

Handel Why should I? It is not what I do. It is what you do.

Susannah But you do. In the music. When I sing your music – the music you write for a woman to sing – there is pain, and sorrow. But there is also such beauty. In the dark, there is light. It overwhelms me, it raises me up, and I feel something else pouring through me, and out of me. I know you feel that too. But there is also something else, which I do not understand; there is a kind of silence, at its heart –

Handel That silence, is what you sing into.

Finally:

It is not that I should not take pleasure in a lover's arms, but I should need it only in order to go on writing.

Silence.

Have you prepared the part we agreed?

Susannah I have. It is very beautiful.

Handel I hope so! It is the final aria. So:

She prepares, and sings, and it is glorious.

Susannah

'If God be for us, who can be against us? Who shall
lay anything to the charge of God's Elect. It is God
that justifieth. Who is he that condemneth?'

Handel is deeply moved.

SCENE SIXTEEN

Crazy Crow (*announcing, in various voices (newspaper
sellers, etc.*)

'For Relief of the Prisoners in the several Gaols –'

'And for the Support of Mercer's Hospital in St
Stephen's Street –'

'And of the Charitable Infirmary on the Inns Quay –'

'This Tuesday 13 April will be performed Mr Handel's
New Grand *sacred oratorio*, MESSIAH!'

Today's the day. The doors open at eleven . . . Le toot
Dublin is coming . . . pushing and shoving and squeezing
their competencies of powder and rage into the one
room where the music will happen.

(*Posh.*) 'The Stewards of the Charitable Musical
Society in order to accommodate the pressing numbers
of the audience, request the favour of the ladies not to
come with their vast and ridiculous hoops this day to the
Musick Hall in Fishamble Street; the gentlemen are
desirous to come without their massively extensive forty-
inch or more Spanish swords . . .'

As for me, I shall wait in my place, backstage. Where
the dust gathers, and the rag and bone piles up, and
the alley stinks. And I swear: I will not listen. I *cannot* ·
listen . . .

SCENE SEVENTEEN

Fishamble Street Musick Hall.

Off: sounds of orchestra tuning up, and singers warming up.

Handel, in director-zone, with Cavendish following.

Handel Ah, Cavendish, where in hell is Mrs Cibber?

Cavendish She is – well, surely she is in her dressing room?

Handel No she is not in her *verfickte* dressing room, she is, in fact, nowhere to be *found*!

Cavendish Now I am sure she will be here at any moment -

Handel And if she is not? *Verdammte schieze!* It will all be a disaster –

He hurries away.

Cavendish (calling after him) It will all be absolutely wonderful! Well, that's what you have to say, isn't it? I do hope so. Another failure would break his great heart. But where can Mrs Cibber be?

Susannah enters fast. She is terrified.

Oh, thank the Lord: you are here.

Susannah Oh God help me oh God help me oh God help me –

Cavendish Are you quite well, my dear?

Susannah No, I am petrified! I have been weeping and puking all night, oh *God* what was I thinking, why did I ever say 'yes' to this?

66

Now in the background: Avoglio performs perfect
warm-up scales and trills.
Susannah is racing so that Cavendish cannot get a
word in.

Listen to her! Signora Avoglio is like some sort of
performing bird, she is always pitch-perfect, never makes
a mistake! Just wind her up and off she goes. I know she
regards me as a singing tart. The audience will throw
oranges. They shall accuse me of hubris -

Cavendish The audience cannot even spell hubris, Mrs
Cibber. Now, calm yourself. Breathe. Breathe...

Susannah obeys, and breathes . . .

You see? All is well. You are a wonder. A glory. A star.
You are quite, quite wonderful. You make me weep.

Susannah I do?

Cavendish Yes, every time I hear you! Look, I am already
weeping, and you have not yet sung -

Susannah I will do my best. That is all I can do – and if I
am laughed out of town, then so be it.

Cavendish takes her hand.

Cavendish Mrs Cibber. Susannah. I believe in you.
Absolutely. Utterly. You are going to break our hearts.
And we shall love you for it.

He kisses her hand, and gazes into her eyes for a
moment too long.

Susannah What time is it? I must prepare myself -

She hurries off. Cavendish watches her go.
Immediately enter Handel in a state of great
anxiety.

Handel Well? Has she appeared?

Cavendish Of course! She is here, and all is well.

Handel almost collapses with relief.

Handel Grazie a Dio, grazie a Dio...

He recovers himself.

Cavendish The audience is ready.

Handel The auditorium is full?

Cavendish A hundred more than it holds! There is no room to breathe, even the fleas have taken to the ceiling to find space to listen. You have a great audience of every kind of people, Sir. And it is the greatest honour of my life, to be here, in this moment. Thank you, from the bottom of my heart.

They embrace.
Cavendish goes.

Handel kneels and prays in silence. A private moment. His fear and distress are revealed to us.

SCENE EIGHTEEN

The Fishamble Street Musick Hall.
Performance of Part Two of Messiah.
The overture plays, followed by the Chorus:

Chorus
'Behold the Lamb of God that taketh away the sin of the world . . .'

Now Susannah steps forward. Silence. The music strikes up. And Susannah sings the whole aria:

68

Susannah

'He was despised, despised and rejected. Rejected of men, a man of sorrows and acquainted with grief.'

Handel watches her, and she knows he's watching, and she sings as she has never sung before, and she breaks our hearts.

SCENE NINETEEN

Fishamble Street Musick Hall, backstage.
Crazy Crow, listening . . . Overcome.

Crazy Crow What the feck is this trickling at my eyes? Am I sick? Do I need a whiskey? A sneeze? A shite? What is this appalling welling? It is the rising of some tide so long gone out of me since I was a boy that I've felt ever since like Donabate Strand on a drizzly winter dawn, the world a horizon of grey, and we poor creatures just the dregs, the broken bottles and tin cans, the flotsam and whatsam of time . . . But now, that tide has returned, and it rises up in my chest until I feel as beauteous and light as Killiney Bay on a vast summer day – and it is glorious and it is cruel, because it hurts, and the stone of my heart like a speckled blue egg has cracked, and up flies some class of a seabird – crying and taking wing, up and away over the glittering waters, calling into the light . . . And I blink, and she's gone, and I am here again. My face wet. Sobbing like a boy. I feel that lost coin again, here –

He holds his hand to his heart.

But I feel something else . . .

And then Susannah and the Chorus sing the end of the 'Amen chorus'.

Chorus
    'Amen' . . .

And in the silence at the end, Handel takes his bow,
bringing Susannah with him.

SCENE TWENTY

Fishamble Street Musick Hall.
    Chorus become the audience leaving. Crazy Crow
among them, becoming the people he describes:

Crazy Crow And it was a vast success. The Bishop of
Elphin was ecstatic.

Edward Synge (*Bishop of Elphin*) Oh sweet Jesus! I
must not blaspheme, but between ourselves the whole
is beyond anything I had a notion of! It seems to be a
species of musick different from any other!

Crazy Crow And the two Dublin newspapers contrived
to out-superlative each other:

Dublin Journal / News Letter (*fighting for phrases*)
'Words are wanting to express the exquisite delight the
work afforded to the admiring crowded audience. The
Sublime, the Grand, and the Tender, adapted to the most
elevated, majestic and moving words, conspired to
transport and charm the ravished heart and ear.'

Crazy Crow And of course the feckin' poets had to get a
word in arseways:

Poet (*terrible recitation*) What can we offer more in
Handel's praise? Since his Messiah gain'd him groves of
bays? Groves that can never wither nor decay, whose
vistas his ability display . . .'

Crazy Crow Ah feck off! And that was that. The takings amounted to a fortune. So that's a fair share of a fortune to each of the charities, and ensuring the release of well more than a hundred debtors. Hallelujah.

Beat.

Now everyone has gone. The applause has died away. Silence . . . And a man stands still, alone, listening . . .

SCENE TWENTY-ONE

Fishamble Street Musick Hall.
  In the empty auditorium after the concert: Handel alone, listening to the silence for a significant period of time.
  Susannah finds him, overjoyed at her triumph. He hides his feelings. She embraces him, and whirls him round.

Susannah Oh I feel . . . I feel like screaming!

Handel Do you –

  She emits a little scream, for joy.

Splendid.

Susannah Are you not ecstatic?

Handel (*ironic*) As you see . . .

Susannah After such a triumph, you should feel . . .

Handel Triumphant?

Susannah Yes!

Handel (*hands up*) And yet . . .

Susannah Enjoy this moment. Please.

  Enter Cavendish, radiant with congratulations.

Cavendish (*to Susannah*) You were absolutely marvellous. People were sobbing! You broke every heart.

Susannah I believe I might have done!

Cavendish Did you hear, as you came to the conclusion of 'He was despised', a gentleman called out: 'Woman, for this be all thy sins forgiven'?

Susannah Did he?

Cavendish Well, that was Dr Delany, the Chancellor of St Patrick's –

Handel Oh a clergyman – absolution indeed . . .

Cavendish You touched his heart – and he a man in mourning for his wife. And that is the power of your music, Sir. You redeem us. You return us to life.

Handel can't reply.

Speaking of wives, mine calls us to a celebration feast –

He exits.

Susannah What will you do now?

Handel A second performance of *Messiah* at the start of June, to replenish my own funds – if you are available?

Susannah Of course. I too shall have a benefit. And then, I will return to London.

Handel To William. And your daughter. You miss them.

Susannah Very much. But everything has changed, because of you –

Handel Hush now –

Susannah How can I repay you?

Handel It is I who must somehow repay you.

Did I tell you, I almost died? A few years ago. I woke up one morning, and I couldn't think or use my right hand. I couldn't play, or write, or conduct. The notes became a flock of tiny black birds I could no longer guide or shape, flying in chaos. What was to become of me? Ruin. Despair. Fear. I felt myself falling into the darkest depths. I believe I was quite lunatic. I was persuaded by my doctors to go to the Baths in Aix-la-Chapelle. I had no belief, none at all. But I took the vapours. I stayed in the baths so long the nuns thought I should surely die. And so did I. But then – life returned, as *music*. I played the organ for hours. I was in a trance, an ecstasy. My fingers and hands moved beyond thought, my mind was redeemed and I was healed and reborn – to *music*. But that was not the end. I went back to London, and alas, a second death; everything went wrong – I was out of favour, out of fashion, the opera failed, I was persecuted and almost bankrupt – until I found myself, in my late age, at a dead end. But Mr Jennens sent me his word book of *Messiah*. And then an invitation bought me here, to Dublin, and to you – to your voice, beloved singer. When the heart sings, it cannot dissemble.

He kisses her hand.

By *woman* came the resurrection of the dead, in my case. So: I think the world might tolerate another performance or two of our *Messiah*. I shall produce it in London. You shall sing it again.

Susannah Do you think they will accept me?

Handel *Accept* you? They will *adore* you.

Susannah And we shall be friends.

Handel Yes. We shall.

*He goes in, leaving her alone for a moment. She cries,
a little.*
    *Crazy Crow enters, festooned with instruments
once more. He turns away when he sees her. But she
calls out.*

Susannah What is your name?

Crazy Crow They call me Crazy Crow –

Susannah But what is your real name?

Crazy Crow Ah, well – George!

Susannah George?

Crazy Crow Exactly like his! Ha. That's what my
mother told me, and I'm inclined to believe her.

Susannah You said I hurt you –

Crazy Crow I did? Well, let's just say it was the
excruciation of the setting of the broken bones of an
old heart.

Susannah And is your heart mended now?

Crazy Crow It is cracked, and crazed, and riddled with
grievous memories. But it beats. For now . . .

He goes, then hesitates:

Where does it come from? The music?

Susannah Listen – what do you hear?

*They listen to the silence and tiny sounds of the
auditorium. Crazy Crow listens, but then scoffs.*

Crazy Crow Ah! You're having me on. What am I
supposed to hear? The sweet nothing of the Liffey in its

foul bed? The turd man pushing his dirt cart in the dark?
Celestial angels having a sing-song with the moon?

Susannah Perhaps –

Susannah briefly touches his heart, which affects him.
Then she exits.
Crazy Crow keeps listening . . . And then:

SCENE TWENTY-TWO

Crazy Crow 'What's your real name? George! Exactly
like his'?! Ha. That's my story. Believe me, don't believe
me. Anyway, soon after they left, I was arrested. For the
bodies, you know. The judge says, 'Do you plead guilty
to a too-literal resurrection of the dead?' They locked me
up. *Bang.*

He slams open the trap door.

Whack fol de daddy-o
 There's whiskey in the jar . . .

They left me, with my heart unlocked, and raging. And
when they let me out, what was I supposed to do with it
then, as I carried it about this broken world?

Whack fol de daddy-o
There's whiskey in the jar.

No, not that. They left me – with something. The music.
I hear it, over and over, in my head. And it pains me, and
it bewilders me, and it holds me.

He sings:

Comfort ye. Comfort ye. Comfort ye.

It is sung, is it not, more than ever, in your own far
distant time, and all across the world? Of course it is.
Hallelujah.

Bass

'Behold I tell you a mystery, we shall not all sleep, but we shall all be chang'd, in a moment, in the twinkling of an eye, at the last trumpet . . .'

And the trumpet sounds, as Handel wrote, 'from afar'. . .

Crazy Crow I'll see yous later.

And he disappears into the trap.

End.